New Buffalo
33 N.
New Buffalo

S0-ACC-142

New Buffalo
33 N.
New Buffalo

Celebrate

Christian Festivals

Series editor: Jan Thompson

Jan Thompson

© 1997 Reed Educational & Professional Publishing
Published by Heinemann Library,
an imprint of Reed Educational & Professional
Publishing,
100 North LaSalle, Suite 1010 Chicago, IL 60602
Customer Service Telephone: 88-454-2279
World Wide Web: www.heinemannlibrary.com

All rights reserved. No part of this publication may be
reproduced or transmitted in any form or by any
means, electronic or mechanical, including
photocopying, recording, taping, or any information
storage and retrieval system, without permission in
writing from the publisher.

Designed by Visual Image
Color reproduction by Track QSP
Printed in Hong Kong by
Wing King Tong Company Limited.

02 01 00
10 9 8 7 6 5 4 3 2

**Library of Congress Cataloging-in-Publication
Data**
Thompson, Jan, 1949-
    Christian festivals / Jan Thompson.
        p.   cm. -- (Celebrate)
    Includes bibliographical references and index.
    Summary: Introduces Christian festivals through
quotations from children talking about their
religious lives as well as through information boxes
and extracts from sacred texts.
    ISBN (invalid) 0-431-06961-1 (lib. bdg.)
    1. Fasts and feasts--Juvenile literature.   [1.
Festivals.   2. Christian life.   3. Holidays.
4. Fasts and feasts.]   I. Title.   II. Series:
Celebrate (Crystal Lake, Ill.)
BV43.T55   1997
263'.9--dc21   96-52605
                                                        CIP
                                                        AC

Acknowledgments
The Publishers would like to thank the following for
permission to reproduce photographs.

Popperfoto: p. 4; Jan Thompson: p. 5; Jan Thompson: p. 6;
Ace Photo Agency/Michael Bluestone: p. 6; Jan Thompson:
p. 8; Robert Harding Picture Library: p .10; Ace Photo
Agency: p. 11; The Children's Society: p. 12; Christ
Bowler/Abbey Studios: p. 13; Jan Thompson: p. 14; Jan
Thompson: p. 15; Jan Thompson: p. 16; Zefa Pictures: p. 16;
Barry Lewis/Network Photographers: p. 17; Jan Thompson:
p. 18; Jan Thompson: p. 19; Zefa Pictures: p. 20; Topham
Picturepoint: p. 21; Royal Mail 1994, designed by Yvonne
Gilbert: p. 22; Britstock-IFA Ltd: p. 23; Frank Spooner
Pictures: p. 24; Tony Morrison/South American Pictures: p. 25;
Jan Thompson: p. 26; Stuart Franklin, Pizarro/Magnum
Photos: P. 27; Abbas/Magnum Photos: p. 28; Vika/Impact
Photos: p. 29; Jan Thompson: p. 30; Sonia Halliday
Photographs: p. 31; Jan Thompson: p. 32; Caroline
Penn/Impact Photos; Homer Sykes/Impact Photos: p. 34;
Andes Press Agency: p. 34; Keith Ellis: P. 35; The Bridgeman
Art Library: p. 36; Mike Williams/Mary Glasgow Publications:
p.37; Jan Thompson: p. 38; St Botolph's Project: p. 39;
Cosmos/Impact Photos: p. 40; Telegraph Colour Library: p.
41; Sonia Halliday Photographs: p. 42; Frank Spooner
Pictures: p. 43

Cover photograph © Zefa Pictures

Details of written sources
Christingle hymn, Come and Praise 1, No. 29, BBC
Publications: p. 13; Carol, Hymns Ancient and Modern
Revised, No. 432, Hymns Ancient and Modern Ltd: p. 17;
Harvest song, Hymns Ancient and Modern Revised, No. 483,
Hymns Ancient and Modern Ltd: p. 38; Hymn, Hymns
Ancient and Modern Revised, No. 525, Hymns Ancient and
Modern Ltd: p. 43; Acts 2:1-4, Good News Bible, The Bible
Societies and Collins, a division of Harper Collins: p. 36

Our thanks to Denise Cush and the Reverend Richard
Meyer for their comments in the preparation of this book.

**Every effort has been made to contact copyright holders of
any material reproduced in this book. Any omissions will be
rectified in subsequent printings if notice is given to the
Publisher.**

Contents

Introduction

*Each year on Easter Sunday thousands of Roman Catholics gather in St. Peter's Square in Rome. They wait to see the Pope come onto his balcony, where he says a prayer over them to **bless** them. The Pope is the leader of the Roman Catholic Church.*

Christians are people who believe in **God** and follow Jesus Christ. He lived two thousand years ago. Since that time, **Christianity** has become the biggest religion in the world. Christians belong to **churches** where they meet together to worship God. Half the Christians in the world belong to the Roman Catholic Church. This is led by the **Pope** in Rome, in Italy. Many Christians in the United States belong to the Roman Catholic Church. There are many Protestant churches, like the Methodist Church, the Episcopal Church, the Lutheran Church, and the Baptist Church. Many Christians in Eastern Europe and some in the United States belong to Orthodox churches, such as the Russian Orthodox Church. As Christians moved to different parts of the world, they set up their own churches.

Lisa is ten years old. She is a Protestant. Once a month her Sunday School class presents a special program during the main church **service**. Lisa's church is called St. Mary's. This is named after **Mary**, the mother of Jesus Christ.

James and John Greenidge are also ten years old. As you can see, they are twins. James and John belong to a Christian family. They were named after two of Jesus' best friends, who were also brothers. James and John go to a Roman Catholic church, called St Joseph's. This is named after **Joseph**, the husband of Mary.

James and John are **altar** boys at their church. This means that they help the **priest** during the service. You can see them here, by the altar in their church, dressed in the special clothes they wear for the service.

James and John also go to a Catholic elementary school. The priest you see in the photo sometimes goes into their school and leads the worship there.

James and John are altar boys. They help the priest during services.

Holidays

> " I was ten on my last birthday. I used to have parties, but now I go out for the day. My birthday's in August and I'm usually on vacation. Last year we went out to the zoo and in the evening we went out for dinner to a nice restaurant. When we got back from vacation, six of my friends came for a sleep-over. "
>
> *– Lisa*

Holidays are happy times that we share with family and friends. Often there are presents and cards and lots of good things to eat. We celebrate together to remember events such as birthdays and anniversaries. Religions also have holidays to remember important events.

Children celebrating at a birthday party

Religious holidays

Christians have lots of holidays. Many of these holidays remind them of important events in the life of Jesus Christ. His birth is remembered at **Christmas** and his death at **Easter**. Some holidays celebrate important events in the history of the **church**, like the birthday of the church at **Pentecost**. Saints' Days, which are celebrated throughout the Catholic Church, recall the lives of special Christians.

People remember important events from long ago because this helps them to think about their own lives now. For instance, when Christians remember that Jesus was born among poor people, they are reminded to help poor people today.

The Christian year

Look at the Christian calendar. You will notice that it starts in December, not January, and each section cuts across our months of the year. The church's year is based on its holidays.

ADVENT is the time when Christians prepare for Christmas.
CHRISTMAS celebrates the birth of Jesus Christ.
EPIPHANY remembers the story of the Wise Men, who found Jesus when he was still a baby.
LENT is when Christians prepare for Easter.
EASTER remembers the death and **resurrection** of Jesus Christ.
ASCENSION celebrates the return of Jesus to **heaven**.
PENTECOST marks the coming of the Holy Spirit to the first Christians, and the beginning of the church.

Calendar colors

The church uses different colors for different times of the year. Purple is for the coming of Christ and his passion, or death and suffering. White is for the times of celebrating, such as Christmas. Red is for Pentecost or **Whitsunday**, to stand for the fire of the Holy Spirit. Red is also used on Saints' Days, for the blood of those who died for their **faith**. Green is used in the weeks after Pentecost. It is the color of growth, when Christians should be growing in their faith.

This book will tell you about some of the Christian holidays. It will tell you about some of the ways Christians around the world celebrate them. It will also help you to understand why they are important for Christians today, even when they are remembering events from long ago.

A diagram of the Christian calendar

7

Advent

Every year I get an Advent calendar. I have one and my little brother Nathan has one. We keep them in the kitchen, out of Nathan's reach because last year he opened all the windows in one day. We're supposed to open one a day. It's like a countdown for Christmas.

– Lisa

An Advent wreath

When is Advent?

Advent is the beginning of the church's year. Advent means "the coming of Christ." It might seem strange to have a new year in December, when January 1 is New Year's Day. But then, we have other new years at different times. For example, the new school year starts in August or September.

Advent **Sunday** is the Sunday nearest to the beginning of December. This is the beginning of Advent. It lasts right through December until Christmas Day on the twenty-fifth.

Making preparations

Advent is a time when **Christians** prepare themselves for Christmas. This does not just mean buying presents and food. They prepare themselves by reading the **Bible** and **praying** at **church** and at home. They think about the difference Jesus made by coming into the world. They make a special effort to live the way Jesus taught people to live.

Counting the days

Many churches use an Advent wreath. This is a circle of evergreens with four colored candles in the middle and one big white candle in the very center. On Advent Sunday, one colored candle is lit at the beginning of the church **service**. On the next Sunday, two candles are lit. This happens on each of the four Sundays in Advent until all four colored candles are lit. On Christmas Day the big white candle is also lit. The big white candle stands for Jesus Christ, who is called the Light of the World. Christians use this symbol because they believe that Jesus brightened up the world by bringing goodness and hope.

Some Christians use an Advent candle in their homes. This is a big candle marked off for 24 days. On each day of December the candle is lit for about half an hour until it burns down to the next date. The candle lasts until Christmas Day.

The Advent calendar, the Advent wreath, and the Advent candle are all ways of counting off the days until Christmas. Christmas is such an important festival that Christians look forward to it all through the four weeks of Advent.

An Advent candle

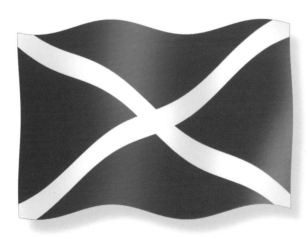

The Scottish flag

St. Andrew

*St. Andrew was one of the earliest followers of Jesus. He was one of his 12 **disciples**. He was a fisherman from Galilee, the brother of Simon-Peter. St. Andrew is the **patron saint** of Scotland. The Scottish flag has the X-shaped cross of St. Andrew on it. St. Andrew's Day is November 30.*

St. Lucia's Day

> **It was my little sister's turn to be St. Lucia this year. Elsa is only four years old, so Mom helped us. She lit the candles only for a little while. She was afraid Elsa would get burned.**
>
> *– Britt*

St Lucia buns

Swedish girl dressed as St Lucia

St. Lucia buns

St. Lucia buns are made from sweet bread dough with a few raisins in it. They are colored yellow with saffron. Once upon a time saffron was a very expensive spice. It was hard to get, so it was only used on very special occasions. The bread dough is pulled into different shapes before it is baked.

What happens on St. Lucia's Day

Swedish-Americans celebrate Saint Lucia's Day on December 13. In Sweden this is like the beginning of **Christmas**. It is celebrated everywhere: in schools, **churches**, stores, and offices. They have processions where a girl is dressed as a Lucia queen or bride. She wears a long white dress and a red sash or belt. On her head is a crown of evergreen leaves and lighted candles. Other girls also dress in white and hold a candle each. The boys are called "star boys," and they wear cone-shaped hats made from thin cardboard and decorated with paper stars. They all sing special **carols** and give out ginger cookies. In some churches the choir dresses up for the procession.

In Swedish homes, often the youngest daughter of a family dresses up as St. Lucia. She is supposed to make breakfast in bed for the rest of the family. They all enjoy coffee and yellow St. Lucia buns.

Who was St. Lucia?

We do not know much about St. Lucia. She was an early **Christian martyr**. This means that she died because of her beliefs. The white dress may stand for her holiness, and the red sash for her death. Many legends have grown up about her. One legend tells how she helped the Christians who were hiding in the tunnels under Rome in Italy. She found her way through the dark tunnels by wearing candles on her head, a bit like a miner's cap. Another legend says that at a time of great hunger in Sweden she miraculously appeared and fed people.

Light and decorations

Saint Lucia is the **patron saint** of light, so people celebrate her day by lighting candles. This day happens in the middle of winter. December is the darkest month of the year in Sweden. Even before the time of Jesus, people celebrated midwinter holidays with light. They wanted to brighten up the long, dark days. They also decorated their homes with evergreens, like holly and fir trees. These things were living when everything else in nature seemed to be dead. They gave them hope that spring would come again with lighter days, and everything would start growing again.

Some of these old customs have now become part of Christmas celebrations. Here in the United States people decorate their homes with trees and lights. You will find other Christian customs that started before **Christianity**. Often they have been given new meanings through their acceptance within the Christian Church.

Christmas tree lit up with candles

Christingle

> **At the Christingle service we have oranges and there are candies stuck into them on sticks. We don't eat the candies at the service, but we eat them afterwards. The lights are switched off so that the church is dark when the candles in the oranges are lit.**
> — *John*

The **Christingle** is a **Christian** symbol of God's gifts to the world. Some British Christians celebrate this holiday around **Christmas**.

- The orange stands for the world that **God** has created.
- The four cocktail sticks stand for the four seasons of the year.
- The fruit, nuts, and candies stand for the fruits of the earth.
- The red ribbon stands for God's love in sending Jesus to the earth.
- The candle stands for Jesus Christ, the Light of the World.
- The word *Christingle* means "Christ-light."

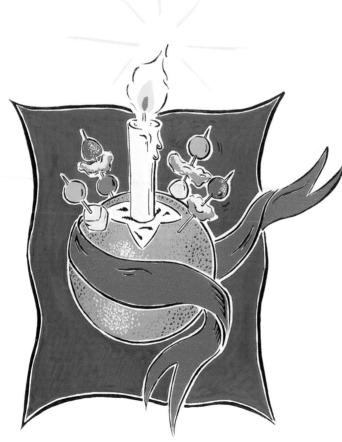

This picture from The Children's Society in Great Britain shows a Christingle.

The history of Christingle
The first Christingle **service** was held in Germany in 1747. The **minister** gave the children Christingles to take home, and told them to put them in their windows. This would remind people that Jesus was the Light of the World. Over 200 years later, in 1968, Christingle services were started again in England by The Children's Society.

| Children with lighted Christingles at a Christingle service

Christingle today

Christingle services are now enjoyed by thousands of people in England, every year. They have songs, readings, and prayers on the theme of light. Money is collected at these services for the work of the Children's Society. This **charity** belongs to the Church of England (Episcopal Church). It helps children in need.

A Christingle service is usually held around Christmastime. As this is the winter season in the northern hemisphere, it is a good time for Christians to think of Jesus as the Light of the World. Also, the service is to thank God for his gifts. Christians believe that God's greatest gift was Jesus himself.

A Christingle hymn

This is the chorus and one verse from a Christian **hymn** on the theme of light. This might be sung at a Christingle service.

From the darkness came light,
from the blackest of nights.
Wait for the morning, the sunlight,
the dawning.
From the darkness came light.

Jesus was born in a stall,
born to bring light to us all.
He came to love us,
a new life to give us;
Jesus was born in a stall.

Nativity Services

Middle Eastern shepherds watching their grazing sheep. They still find shelter in caves in the hills. Jesus was probably born in such a cave.

In the **Bible** there are two accounts of the birth of Jesus. There is one in St. Matthew's **Gospel** and one in St. Luke's Gospel. Luke tells us that Jesus was born in a stable in **Bethlehem**, and that shepherds came to visit him on that first **Christmas** night.

Nativity scenes

A Nativity scene or Christmas crèche is a model of the stable where Jesus was born. It has the figures of **Mary** and Joseph, the baby Jesus laid in a manger, and some shepherds. It also has model animals like sheep, a donkey, and cattle. The custom started with St. Francis of Assisi nearly 800 years ago. One Christmas Eve he recreated a life-sized scene of Jesus' birth in a cave for the villagers nearby. They found that it helped them to imagine what the first Christmas must have been like. The idea spread from Italy, but with smaller models instead.

Blessing the crèche

Nativity scenes are set up in many **churches** to remind people of the story of Jesus' birth. In some church communities, there is a special **service** for the **priest** or minister to **bless** the crèche. Here are some words from the prayers that the priest might use:

"Bless this crèche which we have prepared to celebrate that **holy** birth. May all who see it be strengthened in **faith**."

*This girl is kneeling in front of a Christmas crèche. Some of the characters from the Nativity are missing—the Wise Men. We hear about the wise men in Matthew's Gospel. These are added to the crèche after Christmas, at **Epiphany**. This is when the Wise Men are remembered by the church.*

Mincemeat pies

Some people eat mincemeat pies at Christmas. They are round pastry cases, filled with sweet mincemeat and covered with a pastry lid. Originally, they were not round but oval in shape. The mincemeat then really was meat. They had no lids, but a small piece of pastry was laid across the top. This was meant to look like a tiny cradle for the baby Jesus.

Have you ever had mincemeat pies at home? Try making some oval ones, half-covered with pastry—like a cradle.

Christmas carols

" I go with my Sunday School class at St. Mary's into the main church sanctuary for the annual carol service. We practice singing all the carols before the service. Normally the children put on a nativity play for the parents to watch. That tells the story of Jesus' birth. "
– *Lisa*

Carols are religious songs. In modern times, the word *carol* has come to mean a song about the "good news" of Christ's birth. Many carols are hundreds of years old. Others are new. They often have a dance rhythm to them, which is not surprising because the word *carol* originally meant "to dance in a circle."

Carol singers collecting money

Where to hear carols

Carols can be heard almost everywhere at Christmas time. They are played in stores and on the radio. They are sung in some schools and in churches. People go out carol-singing in groups. You may see them at busy places like supermarkets. Or they may come knocking on your door. Sometimes they collect money at the same time to give to charity.

On Christmas Eve in England, there is a special carol service on television. This comes from the beautiful **chapel** of King's College at Cambridge University. This Service of Nine Lessons and Carols started there over 75 years ago. Many churches around the world now use the same service. The lessons are readings from the **Bible**, the **Christian** holy book. They were chosen to tell the story of **God's** love for the world, ending with Jesus' birth. Carols are sung between each reading.

The carols

This grand service in King's College always starts with one choirboy singing a solo. He sings the first verse of the carol "Once in Royal David's City." Several choirboys are prepared for this, and the boy who is chosen is only told just before the service!

Some verses from "Oh Little Town of Bethlehem" are opposite. Bethlehem is where King **David** of the Old Testament was born. Jesus was also born here.

Phillips Brooks, a Boston rector, wrote "Oh Little Town of Bethlehem" in 1865.

A carol

Oh little town of Bethlehem,
How still we see thee lie.
Above thy deep and dreamless sleep
The silent stars go by.
Yet in thy dark streets shineth
The everlasting light.
The hopes and fears of all the years
Are met in thee tonight.

How silently, how silently,
The wondrous gift is given.
So God imparts to human hearts
The blessings of his heaven.
No ear may hear his coming—
But in this world of sin
Where meek souls will receive
    him still,
The dear Christ enters in.

Choirboys at the carol service from King's College, Cambridge

17

Christmas Eve

> We've only been once to Midnight Mass. I thought it was going to be good at first, going to church in the middle of the night. But it was a very long Mass and I just felt tired. I was serving at the altar and I nearly fell asleep.
>
> *– John*

Christmas Eve services

Many churches hold services on Christmas Eve. Some common names for these sevices are "Lessons and Carols," "Candlelight Communion," and "Midnight Mass." Mass or Communion is a special church service where bread and juice or wine are used to stand for the body and blood of Jesus. Christians feel very close to Jesus when they eat the bread and drink the juice or wine.

Christmas pilgrims

A **pilgrim** is a religious person who travels to a **holy** place. Many Christians travel to Israel at **Christmas** time. They crowd into Manger Square in **Bethlehem** on Christmas Eve. This is outside the Church of the **Nativity**. The famous bells here ring out at midnight and are shown on televisions around the world.

Christian pilgrims to Bethlehem can go down some steps into a cave under the church. In the floor is a star marking the place where it is believed Jesus was born. It is a custom for the pilgrims to kneel down and kiss the star.

The story of Jesus' birth

Luke's **Gospel** tells us that **Mary** and her husband **Joseph** traveled south to Bethlehem to register for the Roman taxes. Mary was pregnant at the time. She had been told by an **angel** that her son would be the Christ, the long-awaited **Savior.** No sooner had they arrived in Bethlehem, than Mary felt her baby coming. But Bethlehem was packed with travelers, and they could not find anywhere to stay. In the end, they had to make do with a stable. They made a cradle for the newborn baby out of the animals' feeding trough, called a manger. The story goes that there were shepherds out on the hills looking after their sheep. Suddenly an angel appeared to them. He told them that the Savior had been born and was lying in a manger. The shepherds set off to find him.

This story teaches Christians about Jesus, who is called the Son of **God**. They might have expected their Lord to be born in luxury, not in a stable. They might have expected kings to be told of his birth, not ordinary shepherds on the nightshift. This teaches Christians that God knows what it is like to be poor, and he cares for ordinary people. It teaches Christians that they, too, must care for the poor and needy.

The star on the floor in the cave under the church in Bethlehem where Jesus is supposed to have been born

Christmas Day

" **Last year Nathan woke me up at one o'clock in the morning. He wanted to open his presents, but I said it was too early. We woke up again at about seven o'clock. We had presents.**
— *Lisa* "

A child on Christmas morning

Christmas card showing a dove—a symbol of peace and the Holy Spirit

The Christmas tradition

Christmas is a very popular holiday. It is usually a family occasion. **Christians** are celebrating the birth of Jesus their **Savior**, and they want to share their happiness with others. It is especially popular with children, who get lots of presents. It was traditional to leave out Christmas stockings to be filled with presents. There are different traditions around the world about who brings the presents. Here in the United States children call him Santa Claus. In Germany, it is said to be the child Jesus. British children say that Father Christmas comes down the chimney with their presents. In Austria and Czechoslovakia it is said to be Saint Nicholas.

Christmas Day in church

Churches usually have **services** on Christmas morning. Everyone wishes each other "Merry Christmas" as they go in. They sing Christmas **carols** instead of the usual **hymns**. The collection on Christmas Day is often given to a **charity**, to help people in need. People are usually very generous because they want to say "thank you" to **God** for all the good things they enjoy at Christmas.

Christmas cards

Apart from presents, people also send each other Christmas cards. This custom started about a hundred years ago, and is now very popular. Cards are a way of keeping in touch with friends and family, and of wishing people a merry Christmas, and a happy New Year. There are many different designs on Christmas cards. Some are winter scenes; some show presents and Christmas dinners. Many Christians like to send cards which show the religious meaning of Christmas. These cards might show the birth of Jesus, or they might have a symbol on them. The dove, for example, is a symbol of peace. Christians believe that Jesus was born to bring peace on earth.

St. Nicholas

*Little is known about St. Nicholas, who was an early **bishop** of the Christian Church. The famous legend about him tells how he saved three girls who were so poor that they could not afford to marry. At night, he secretly left them three bags of gold. St. Nicholas is the **patron saint** of children, and is supposed to bring them presents. "St. Nicholas" is another name for Santa Claus.*

Why is Christmas in December?

Christmas is celebrated every year on December 25, but no one knows exactly when Jesus was born. The church chose this date over 300 years after his birth. Winter is a good time for Christians to celebrate the birth of Jesus, who is known as the Light of the World, and Christians find that Jesus gives them hope at the darkest, saddest times in their lives.

Of course, when Christians settled in the southern hemisphere, Christmas came in the summer. Many Australians have a Christmas barbecue on the beach and hold open-air Christmas processions.

An open-air Christmas procession in Australia

Epiphany

" **Epiphany is on January 6 and it's when the Wise Men came to see Jesus. We have the Wise Men in our Sunday School Nativity play, which is performed in the church. They come up the center of the church, then we all sing the carol "We Three Kings."**

– Lisa **"**

Where the Wise Men are described

There are two **nativity** stories in the **Bible.** Luke's **Gospel** tells the story of the **angels** and the shepherds at Jesus' birth. The story of the Wise Men comes from Matthew's Gospel. The two stories are usually joined together in school Nativity plays, but they ought to be kept separate.

The story of the wise men is celebrated in church twelve days after **Christmas**, at **Epiphany**. This is a Greek word which means "to make known."

Children dressed as the Wise Men on a British Christmas stamp, 1994

The Wise Men's gifts

The gifts of the Wise Men are important. Each was a symbol that teaches Christians about Jesus. Gold was for a king, and Christians call Jesus the King of Kings. Frankincense was used in worship, and Christians worship Jesus Christ. Myrrh was a perfume which was put on dead bodies, and Jesus was to die. For the past 700 years in England, these three gifts have been presented at the **altar** of the **Chapel** Royal in St. James' Palace in London by a member of the British royal family. In Spain, Epiphany is when children get lots of presents, rather than at Christmas. They write letters to the Three Kings to tell them what they would like. There are big processions, with three men dressed up as the kings.

Spanish Twelfth Night (Epiphany) celebrations. Christians think of the Wise Men as three kings.

The story of the Wise Men

Soon after Jesus was born, some Wise Men arrived in **Jerusalem**. They had come from the east because they had seen a special star. It meant that a new king was born. They asked at King Herod's palace in Jerusalem, but Herod knew nothing of a new king. He was worried by the news. Who was this new king? Would he grow up to take Herod's throne? There was a passage in the Bible which said that a leader of the Jews would come from **Bethlehem**. So Herod sent the Wise Men to the little town of Bethlehem, a few miles south of Jerusalem. He asked them to tell him if they found the king,

so that he could come and worship him too. In fact, all he wanted to do was to kill this new king, because he saw him as a threat. When the Wise Men found the child Jesus in Bethlehem, they worshiped him and gave him their presents of gold, frankincense, and myrrh. They did not tell Herod. They had been warned in a dream, and went home another way. Herod was so angry that he sent his soldiers to Bethlehem to kill all the boys under the age of two. But he did not kill Jesus. **Mary** and **Joseph** had already taken him to Egypt, where they stayed until Herod's death.

Lent

> **We have a special Mass on Ash Wednesday. You have to go up to the front of the church and Father just dips his hand in a bowl of ashes and puts a cross on your forehead.**
>
> *– John*

> **Ash Wednesday is the beginning of Lent. We give up candy during Lent. Well, I say I do, but I can't!**
>
> *– James*

A pancake race in Great Britain

What is Lent?

Lent is celebrated by many churches. It is a time of 40 days before **Easter** (not counting **Sundays**). Its name simply refers to the time of year when the days begin to lengthen with the coming of spring. The Lenten season starts with Ash Wednesday. Ashes are a symbol of sorrow for one's wrongdoing. Lent is a time when **Christians** prepare for Easter by thinking about the things they have done wrong. We all make mistakes, we sometimes hurt other people, and we can feel disappointed with ourselves. Christians believe that **God** forgives their sins and gives them a fresh start if they are really sorry.

Giving things up for Lent

Christians used to **fast** during Lent. Fasting means giving up food. They did this because Jesus spent 40 days in the desert without food. Some Christians still fast or give up things like candy during Lent. Some try to do something extra for God at this time, like reading the **Bible** every day, or saving for a

charitable organization in a special Lenten folder.

Shrove Tuesday

The day before Lent starts is called **Shrove Tuesday**, because people used to go to church to be "shriven" on that day. This means they confessed their sins to a **priest** and were forgiven. Shrove Tuesday is also called Pancake Day in England, or Mardi Gras in France. Pancakes were eaten on this day to use up all the rich foods before Lent. Many British people still eat pancakes on Shrove Tuesday and some run in pancake-races.

Carnivals

Carnivals also take place at this time. The word *carnival* means "take away meat," and it was a chance to celebrate together before the serious time of Lent. One such carnival in the U.S. is Mardi Gras, which takes place in New Orleans, Louisiana.

A Caribbean carnival

Mothers' Day

Americans celebrate Mothers' Day on the second Sunday in May, but many Christians celebrate it in the middle of Lent, on the fourth Sunday. It began as a religious festival. Some churches have little bunches of spring flowers for the children to give to their mothers. In church, special prayers are said for mothers, like this one:

"Heavenly Father, we thank you for our mothers. They are very special to us because they gave us birth. Thank you for all the love they have given us. Thank you for all their hard work in bringing us up. Help us always to love them in return.

Amen."

Palm Sunday

> **The priest carries a big palm branch in church on Palm Sunday. And he gives you a palm cross. That was to remember when Jesus came to Jerusalem and they chopped down palms and laid them down for him.**
>
> *– James*

> **Dad's from Barbados and we go every two years. I've seen palm trees there.**
>
> *– John*

These children have made palm branches out of card and paper at Sunday School. They had their own procession through the churchyard. Can you see the small palm crosses they are also holding?

What is Palm Sunday?

Palm Sunday celebrates Jesus' arrival at **Jerusalem** for the Jewish festival of Passover. Many people must have hoped that Jesus was the **Savior** who was promised to them in the **Bible**. This is what they did: "The next day the large crowd that had come to the Passover Festival heard that Jesus was coming to Jerusalem. So they took branches of palm trees and went out to meet him, shouting, 'Praise **God**! God **bless** him who comes in the name of the Lord! God bless the King of Israel.'" (John 12:12–13 Good News Bible)

■ *Palm trees*

A Palm Sunday procession in Latin America with a statue of Jesus on a donkey

Palm Sunday processions

In many parts of the United States and in warm countries, particularly Roman Catholic countries, the Palm Sunday procession often takes place out in the streets. Sometimes a live donkey is used in the procession with a statue of Jesus on it. This is because Jesus rode into Jerusalem on a donkey, to show that he came in peace, and to fulfill **Old Testament** prophecy. If you look at the hair on a donkey's back, you will see that it forms the shape of a cross. Folklore says it has been there ever since Jesus rode into Jerusalem on a donkey, because it was there that he died on a cross.

Palm crosses

Palm Sunday is both a happy and a sad occasion. **Christians** are happy because they are singing Jesus' praises. But they are also sad because they know that Jesus died on a cross less than a week after he had entered Jerusalem. So Christians are given little palm crosses on Palm Sunday, made from single palm leaves. It is the beginning of **Holy Week**, the last week of **Lent**. This is a very special week for Christians, as they read in the Bible about the last few days of Jesus' life. Many churches have **services** every day this week.

The palm crosses that are left over are kept for almost a year. Then they are burned and their ashes are used on **Ash Wednesday** to put on people's foreheads on the first day of Lent.

Maundy Thursday

❝ **At the service on Maundy Thursday twelve men go up and have their feet washed. My Dad's usually one of them. The priest washes their feet.** ❞

– James

The Last Supper

On the night before his death, Jesus ate a final meal with his **disciples**. This is called the Last Supper. At that meal, he took the bread and the wine and gave them a whole new meaning. He said that the bread was his body, and the wine was his blood. Jesus must have known that he would soon be taken away from them. He wanted to leave them something to remember him by. Throughout history **Christians** have shared bread and wine together to remember Jesus. It is done at a special **church service**. This has various names such as **Mass**, **Holy Communion**, the **Eucharist**, and the Lord's Supper. Not all churches do this, but for those that do, it is their most important service. The Holy Communion service that Christians attend on the Thursday evening in Holy Week is extra special. It is a time to remember how it all began on the night before Jesus died.

A priest blesses the bread and wine at Holy Communion

What is Maundy Thursday?

The Thursday in Holy Week is called **Maundy Thursday.** *Maundy* means a mandate or command. John's **Gospel** records a new command that Jesus gave his followers on this night. It was that they should love one another as he loved them. He showed them how much he loved them by washing their feet. This was the servant's job. By doing it himself, Jesus was teaching his disciples that none of them should be too proud to look after one another.

Sometimes, at the Maundy Thursday service, the priest will wash the feet of 12 people from the church. The **Pope** washes the feet of 12 choirboys in St Peter's cathedral in Rome. In Britain, the monarch no longer washes the feet of 12 poor people, but the Queen gives out special Maundy money to a group of elderly retired people.

Some Christian churches in the United States celebrate Maundy Thursday with a foot-washing ceremony. Foot washing is done in Pentecostal churches at other times of year as well. They do it at their **Sunday** service, to show their love for one another.

Maundy Thursday evening

After the Last Supper, Jesus went with his disciples to the Garden of Gethsemane on the Mount of Olives. Before the soldiers came to arrest him, he had asked his disciples to stay awake with him while he **prayed**. Today, Christians often remember this by staying in church for an extra hour after the service is over on the evening of Maundy Thursday. Some may stay even longer in silent prayer.

Jesus was kept in prison on Thursday night. The next day, the Jews handed him over to Pilate, the Roman governor.

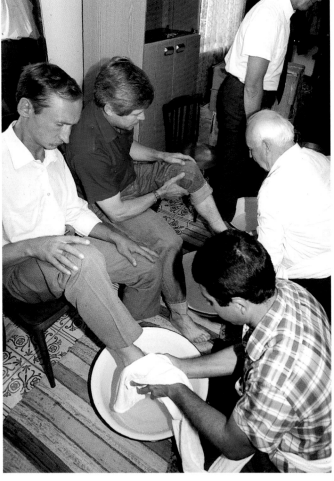

A foot-washing service

Good Friday

" At Sunday School we took a moment of silence to think about Jesus' death—how he died and why he died. We had paper to write down our ideas. Some people thought the religious leaders wanted to kill him because they thought he was telling lies about being God's son. But most of us thought he died because he wanted to die for other people to live. He was caring. "

– Lisa

The fifth Station of the Cross shows Simon helping Jesus carry the cross.

What is Good Friday?

In many ways, **Good Friday** is not good at all. It is the day when **Christians** remember Jesus' death. It is thought that the name may have started as "God's Friday" rather than "Good Friday."

The Stations of the Cross

In Catholic **churches** you can see 14 pictures, or plaques, around the walls. These are called the **Stations of the Cross.** They tell the story of the final hours of Jesus' life on the first "Good Friday." They start with his trial in front of Pilate, the Roman governor and finish with his burial. They are called *stations* because this means a stopping point. Each Station of the Cross was a stopping point on Jesus' final journey to his death. They are also points for Catholic Christians to stop and **pray** about the meaning of Jesus' suffering. For instance, the fifth Station shows a man called Simon being made to help Jesus carry his cross. Christians might pray for strength to help Jesus whenever they are called upon to do so. Christians believe that they can help Jesus today by helping anyone who is in need, because these were the people that Jesus loved.

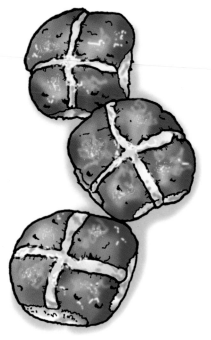

Hot cross buns

Christian **pilgrims** to the **Holy** Land pray at the Stations of the Cross in the Via Dolorosa. This is the winding street along which Jesus carried his cross. Its name means "Way of Sorrows." Often, groups of pilgrims carry a life-sized cross with them.

The symbol of the cross

The cross has become the main symbol for **Christianity**. Some Christians eat hot cross buns on Good Friday, to mark the day when Jesus died on the cross. Many Christians wear crosses as jewelry, or have them hanging on their walls. You can usually see crosses both inside and outside church buildings. There are different shapes and types of crosses, all with their own special meanings. A cross with the figure of Jesus on it is called a **crucifix**. This reminds Christians of Jesus' suffering.

Some Christians go to church on Good Friday morning for a **service** to "venerate" the cross. This means to show it respect. During this sad service, they come up to the front and kiss the crucifix. From noon until 3 o'clock in the afternoon, Christians remember the time that Jesus hung on the cross. Some churches have a three-hour service at this time.

The Via Dolorosa, the road on which Jesus walked to his death on the cross

Easter

> **On Easter Day**
> I watch all the shows about Jesus on television. I read the Bible—it's a children's Bible. And I draw pictures of Jesus—all the different stories I've heard about him. **"**
>
> *– Lisa*

> **Normally I get**
> 10 or 12 chocolate Easter eggs. I don't eat them all at once! **"**
>
> *– Lisa*

What is Easter?

Easter is the most important of all the **Christian** holidays. There is a long buildup to it during the six weeks of **Lent**. During the final week, called **Holy** Week, many **churches** hold **services** every day.

Easter eggs are given on Easter **Sunday**. Easter parades are a tradition in many places, when people wear Easter bonnets.

Easter eggs

Young birds and reptiles hatch from eggs, so Easter eggs are symbols of new life. Also, as they are cracked open, they stand for the empty tomb of Jesus.

At Easter, many children dye eggs or paint them with beautiful patterns.

■ *A bird sitting on its eggs*

The Resurrection

Easter is the time when Christians remember that Jesus died on the cross, was buried, and then started a new life. After the sadness of Good Friday, Christians rejoice together as they celebrate their belief in his **resurrection**. Church buildings are bright with spring flowers, and happy songs are sung, with words like these:

> *"Jesus Christ is risen today.* ***Alleluia.*** *Let shouts of praise and joy outburst. Alleluia."*

Why is Easter so important for Christians? Without the resurrection, Jesus would have been seen only as a great teacher. After the resurrection, Christians called Jesus "my Lord and my **God**."

Greek Orthodox Christians gathered in candlelight at midnight on Easter Eve

Different Easter celebrations

Easter can come on any Sunday between March 21 and April 25. It depends on the full moon during the Jewish Passover. Christians found it difficult to agree when to celebrate Easter. The Western and Eastern Churches still follow a different calendar. Their Easters are sometimes as much as a month apart.

Easter is a very big holiday in Eastern Orthodox countries like Greece. Late on Holy Saturday night, Orthodox Christians gather at church. They will be there to celebrate Christ's resurrection as Easter Day dawns. Just before midnight they go outside with their candles, leaving the church in darkness. At midnight, the cry goes up "Christ is risen," and the people reply "He is risen indeed." They enter the dark, empty church like the first **disciples** coming to the tomb where Jesus had been laid to rest and finding it empty.

Sundays

> **We sing songs to God and have a few prayers. The pastor gives a talk. They read from the Bible, from the Old Testament and the New Testament.**
>
> *– Lisa*

People in church for a Sunday service

People dressed up for church

What makes Sunday different?

Christians believe that Jesus rose from the dead on a **Sunday**, so Sunday is their **holy** day. It is a special day set apart each week for worship. Some Christians attend one **service** on a Sunday. Others spend most of the day on **church** activities. In the past, Sunday was a day of rest in Western countries. Now you can often find stores open. Some Christians still keep Sunday special and different from the rest of the week. All the work around the house is done on Saturday, so that there is time to relax on Sunday with family and friends. On Sundays, people may dress up in nice clothes, which used to be called "Sunday best." The midday meal is traditionally the Sunday dinner, the best meal of the week.

Sunday services

Many churches have more than one service on a Sunday. They usually last an hour. The services are a mixture of **hymns**, prayers, Bible readings, and a **sermon**. About once a month there will also be a special service of **Holy Communion.** Some churches have Communion services more often than this. Many Catholics like to attend **Mass** every Sunday, so there are a number of services provided for them. These services usually last about 45 minutes. There might be one at 8 A.M., 9:30 A.M., 11:15 A.M. and 6 P.M. Many Catholic churches also hold Mass on Saturday evenings for people who cannot get to church on Sundays, perhaps because of their work. Some churches have much longer services. If you go to an Eastern Orthodox Church, the service could well last for several hours.

Sunday schools

*Churches have to cater for all ages, and children may find the services long and boring if they are mainly for the grown-ups. So many churches run Sunday schools for children. Here they can worship God in a children's service and learn about **Christianity.** Sometimes children join in part of the main service, and spend the rest of the time on their own activities, led by Sunday school teachers.*

| Children taking part in the church service

Ascension and Pentecost

"I think the Holy Spirit is the spirit of Jesus in the world. The Holy Spirit makes a difference to me, knowing that you've got somebody to look after you.

– *John*

An artist's idea of Jesus' ascension

Ascension Day

The Easter season in the church lasts for 40 days, and ends with **Ascension** Day. To *ascend* means to go up. Ascension Day is when **Christians** celebrate the end of Jesus' time on earth and his going up into **heaven** while his disciples watched. This story is told in Acts in the New Testament. On Ascension Day, Christians celebrate because they believe that Jesus has authority over everything as King of Kings. When he lived on earth he could only be in one place at a time. Now Christians all over the world believe that Jesus, through the Holy Spirit, hears them when they **pray**.

Pentecost

Ten days after Ascension Day, Christians celebrate **Pentecost**, the feast that marks the end of the 50-day observance of Easter. It is also called **Whitsunday.** Jesus promised his **disciples** that the Holy Spirit of God would give them power to preach about him to the ends of the earth. This happened at the Jewish feast of Pentecost.

"When the day of Pentecost came, all the believers were gathered together in one place. Suddenly there was a noise from the sky which sounded like a strong wind blowing, and it filled the whole house where they were sitting. Then they saw what looked like tongues of fire which spread out and touched each person there. They were all filled with the Holy Spirit . . ."

The coming, or advent, of the Spirit of God was said to be like wind and fire. This is because wind and fire are very powerful and are sources of energy. Wind and fire are used as symbols of the Holy Spirit, because the disciples were given power and energy at Pentecost to go out and preach about Jesus. Many people came to believe in Jesus as their **Savior** on that day. Pentecost is also seen as the beginning of the church.

Christians today pray that the Holy Spirit will give them power to do God's work in the world. Churches see the power of God working among them in different ways. Some claim amazing miracles of healing. Others feel God's spirit working quietly in their hearts, helping them to love and care for people.

How Pentecost is celebrated

Another name for Pentecost is Whitsunday, which comes from "White Sunday." It probably got this name because it was the custom for new Christians to be baptised on this day, wearing white. It is the third most important festival in the church after **Christmas** and Easter. The Roman Catholic Church, the Eastern Orthodox Churches, most Lutheran Churches, and the churches of the Anglican union celebrate the Ressurection of Jesus at this time. In England, some areas have a tradition of decorating local wells to thank God for the water. Well dressing, as it is called, is done by building a wooden frame over or around the well. This is covered in damp clay and pictures are made by sticking natural things into the clay. All sorts of things can be used, like flowers, moss, shells, pebbles and seeds. They are usually religious pictures, showing scenes from the **Bible**.

Well dressing

Harvest Festival

A Harvest Festival hymn

*We plough the fields and scatter
the good seed on the land,
but it is fed and watered
by God's almighty hand.*

*All good gifts around us
are sent from **heaven** above;
then thank the Lord, O thank the Lord,
for all his love.*

> **At Sunday School
we have a Harvest Festival.
We bring in food to
represent the harvest. You
can take anything. After the
service the food is donated
to needy people.**
> – *Lisa*

Christians believe that **God** created the earth. Some Christians celebrate **Harvest** Festivals to thank God for all the good things that come from the earth.

When is Harvest Festival?

Some Harvest Festivals are held at the beginning of harvest time. In Scotland, Lammas is celebrated on August 1. "Lammas" means "loaf mass." A loaf of bread is made from the first wheat that is cut. It is taken to church for the bread which is eaten at **Mass.**

Some Harvest Festivals are held at the end of harvest time. In the Shetland Isles, in Scotland, deep-sea fishing used to end on August 1. So they also gave thanks for the harvest of the sea at Lammas, when all the boats had returned safely with their catch of fish.

Autumn in the northern hemisphere comes between August and October. But it comes between March and May in the southern hemisphere. So this is when Christians in Australia and New Zealand celebrate their Harvest Festivals.

A church decorated for Harvest Festival

How the harvest is celebrated

In Britain, churches often celebrate Harvest Festival in the autumn, when the wheat has been cut and the apples picked. The church is decorated with flowers and greenery. Fruit and vegetables are put on display, with a special loaf of bread in the middle. In some country churches a plow is brought in from a local farm. The **priest** says a blessing over it and **prays** for a good harvest in the year to come.

Why Harvest Festival is special

Harvest Festival reminds Christians of all the good things God gives them. This makes them want to share with others who are not so lucky. After the **service**, the food that has been put on display is usually made into parcels and given to people in need. Some churches make appeals for special things. St. Botolph's Church in the East End of London collects things like soap, towels, tea and sugar. They give these things to the many single homeless people in that area. They ask other churches in and around London to help them with this collection, and stack everything up in the church.

harvest APPEAL

ST BOTOLPH'S PROJECT
Working with people who are homeless

Please help St Botolph's Project in its work with homeless people by bringing:

- Coffee, Teabags & Sugar
- Tinned & Packet Soup
- Flour, Pasta & Rice
- Tinned Fruit & Vegetables
- Biscuits
- Tinned Meat & Fish
- Cleaning Materials
- Soap & Shampoo
- Automatic Washing Powder
- Shaving Foam & Disposable Razors
- Plastic Rubbish Sacks
- Towels & Tea Towels

St Botolph's Project
The Crypt Centre
Aldgate High Street
London EC3N 1AB
Tel: 071 283 1950/1670

A poster from St. Botolph's Church in England, appealing for special Harvest gifts

A priest at St. Botolph's Church surrounded by the canned food that has been given for Harvest

Thanksgiving

" Pumpkin pie is a real favorite with our family. Even though we all like it, we never eat it except at Thanksgiving. That keeps it a special treat for a special holiday.
– Anna "

What is Thanksgiving?

Thanksgiving is one of the most important holidays in the United States. It is observed on the fourth Thursday in November in memory of the first **harvest** of the English settlers in America nearly 400 years ago.

At that time, America was called the New World because it had only just been discovered by Europeans. These first settlers were Puritans. They liked to have a very simple, strict form of **Christianity**, based on the **Bible**. They went to America to start new lives and set up new **churches** where they could worship **God** in their own way.

These Mennonite Christians in Central America still live and dress like the early Puritans.

A family
celebrates
Thanksgiving.

The Pilgrims

The journey across the Atlantic Ocean was very dangerous, but the Puritans made it. They called their settlement Plymouth. These first Puritan settlers are known as the **Pilgrims** and are honored as the founders of the nation. Over the next 20 years 20,000 more Puritans emigrated to North America.

Life was hard for the Pilgrims and almost half of them died during that first winter. But, with the help of Native Americans, they hunted for food and planted crops. On the following year, when their first crops were gathered, they gave special thanks to God because it was proof that they could survive in this new land. This is the origin of Thanksgiving.

How Thanksgiving Day is celebrated

On Thanksgiving Day many families attend a **service** at church. They bring gifts to share with those who cannot afford to have a special meal. Afterwards they go home for a big Thanksgiving meal.

Thanksgiving is an important family occasion. Many families have a huge meal of turkey followed by pumpkin pie for dessert. Turkey is traditional because the early settlers caught wild turkeys to eat. Pumpkins were grown by the early settlers and used as both a vegetable and dessert.

All Saints' Day and Day of the Dead

> **The saints— like St. Mary and St. George—are people that God chose to be special.**
>
> – *Lisa*

> **They have halos around their heads that make them look nice and peaceful and heavenly and special people.**
>
> – *James*

Halloween

The evening before All Saints' Day is known as Halloween. This is because "hallowed" means holy or saintly, so "all hallows" means "all saints."

A statue of Peter, one of Jesus' disciples

Who are saints?

Saints are **holy Christians** who have lived their lives for **God**. This could be said of many Christians, but some churches have named particular people as saints. Many of these saints were Jesus' disciples.

The apostle Peter was one of Jesus' 12 **disciples**. He is known as St. Peter in the Catholic Church. He became the leader of the church after Jesus died. In the statue above, he holds a large key. This is a symbol that he can let people into **heaven**. Peter made lots of mistakes, but Jesus forgave him and still chose him to be the leader. This shows us that saints are not perfect. They are people believed to be chosen by God to do something special for him.

Some Christians lead such saintly lives that people treat them like saints. Mother Teresa of Calcutta is one example. She has devoted her whole life to God and to the care of the poor who are sick and dying.

Saints' days

Many saints were **martyrs**. That means they died for being a Christian. That is why red is used in the church on saints' days. It stands for the blood of the martyrs. Often the saint's day, when that saint is remembered, is the day that he or she died.

All Saints' Day, on November 1, is a chance for the church to celebrate all the saints. The **hymns** that are sung in church on this day often speak of the crowns that the saints wear. One hymn says:

"O may we tread the sacred road
that saints and holy martyrs trod…
and win, like them, a crown of life."

This is a way of showing the Christian belief that the saints are rewarded with eternal life. For the same reason, saints are usually shown with a crown of light around their heads. This is called a **halo**.

Day of the Dead

The day after All Saints' Day is called All Souls' Day. It is when the church **prays** for Christians who have died. In Mexico, it is called the Day of the Dead. It is a national *fiesta* or festival. Skulls made of chocolate and icing are on sale everywhere. There are also cakes in the shape of skulls. People visit the graves of their loved ones who have died and put yellow flowers on them. Offerings for the souls of the dead are set out in public squares and in people's houses. They put out trays of bread, water, fruit and flowers. Many of these customs go back to the very old religion of the native Mexicans before they became **Christians**.

Mother Teresa of Calcutta

Glossary

Advent the time of preparation before Christmas

Alleluia (also "Halleluja") a shout of praise

altar table in a church used for Holy Communion

angel messenger from God

Ascension festival to celebrate the belief that Jesus reigns in heaven

Ash Wednesday the first day of Lent

Bethlehem the town where Jesus was born

Bible the Christian holy book

bishop a leader of a group of ministers

bless to make holy and happy

carol a religious song, usually sung at Christmas

chapel a church building, usually quite small

charity voluntary organization to help the needy

Christian belonging to Christianity

Christianity the religion which follows Jesus Christ

Christingle an orange decorated for a special service; it means "Christ-light"

Christmas festival to celebrate the birth of Jesus Christ

church group of Christians, also the building where they worship

crucifix a cross with the figure of Jesus

David the greatest king of the Jews in Old Testament times

disciple a follower—for example, the twelve disciples of Jesus

Easter festival to celebrate the death and resurrection of Jesus

Epiphany festival to remember that Jesus was sent for the whole world

Eucharist another name for communion; bread is eaten and wine is drunk in remembrance of Jesus

faith belief

fast to go without food

God the all-powerful, supreme being

Good Friday the day Jesus died

Gospel a type of book in the New Testament about the life of Jesus

halo a circle of light around the head

harvest gathering in crops

heaven believed to be where God is and where people go after death

holy set apart for a religious purpose

Holy Communion the service which uses the symbols of bread and wine

Holy Week the week before Easter

hymn a religious song

Jerusalem the city where Jesus died

Joseph the husband of Mary

Lent the time of preparation before Easter

martyr someone who dies witnessing to his or her faith

Mary the mother of Jesus

Mass the service which uses bread and wine, also called Holy Communion

Maundy Thursday the night before Jesus died, when he ate the Last Supper with his disciples

minister a religious leader

Nativity birth

New Testament the last 27 books of the Bible

Old Testament the first 39 books of the Bible

Palm Sunday the Sunday before Easter Sunday; a festival to celebrate Jesus' triumphal entry into Jerusalem

patron saint saint believed to protect a particular place or people

Pentecost the birthday of the church, when the Holy Spirit came upon the first Christians, also called Whitsunday

pilgrim a religious person who travels to a holy place

Pope leader of the Roman Catholic Church, the bishop of Rome

pray to speak and listen to God

priest a religious leader

redeemer savior, used to describe Jesus

resurrection rising from death

saints special, holy people

savior someone who saves people, used to describe Jesus

sermon a religious talk

service an act of worship

Shrove Tuesday the day before Lent starts

Stations of the Cross the 14 stages of Jesus' final journey on Good Friday

Sunday the Christian holy day each week

More Books to Read

Christianity. John Logan; Thomson Learning, 1995.

Christmas Around the World. Judith H. Corwin; Silver Burdett Press, 1995.

Easter. J. Fox; Rourke, 1989.

Let's Celebrate Autumn. Mike Rosen, ed. Deb Elliott; Wayland (Publishers) Ltd., 1994.

Let's Celebrate Summer. Mike Rosen, ed. Deb Elliott; Wayland (Publishers)Ltd., 1994.

Let's Celebrate Winter. Mike Rosen, ed. Deb Elliott; Wayland (Publishers) Ltd., 1994.

Understanding Religions: Food and Fasting. Deidre Burke, Wayland (Publishers) Ltd., 1992.

Understanding Religions: Pilgrimages and Journeys. Katherine Prior, Wayland (Publishers) Ltd., 1992.

A Closer Look

This picture shows a Palm Sunday procession in Latin America with a statue of Jesus on a donkey. Palm Sunday celebrates Jesus' arrival at Jerusalem for the Jewish festival of Passover. Jesus rode on a donkey to show that he came in peace. It is both a happy and sad occasion for Christians, for though they sing Jesus' praises, he died on a cross less than a week after he had entered Jerusalem.

Index

Plain numbers (3) refer to the text. Italic numbers (*3*) refer to a picture.